D1104200

Kids Can Cook

MIDWESTERN
RECIPES

Mary Boone

Mitchell Lane
PUBLISHERS

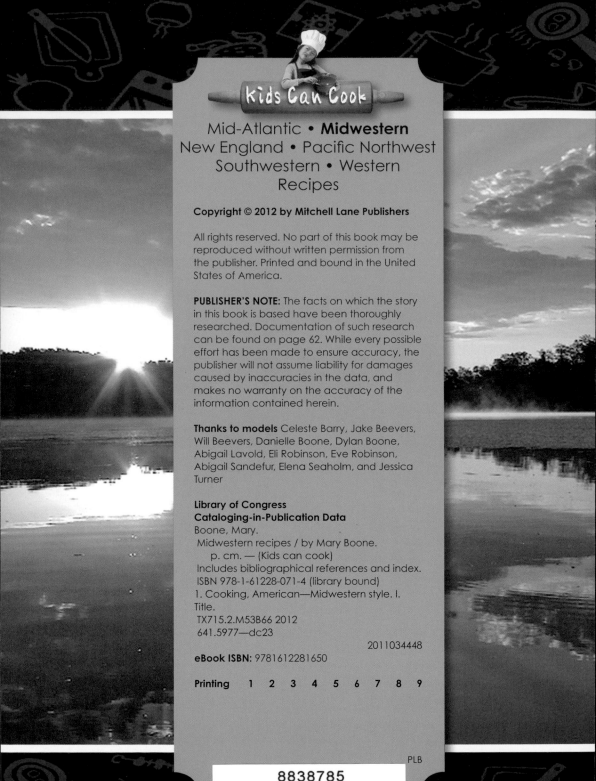

Kids Can Cook

Mid-Atlantic • **Midwestern**
New England • Pacific Northwest
Southwestern • Western
Recipes

Copyright © 2012 by Mitchell Lane Publishers

PUBLISHER'S NOTE: The facts on which the story in this book is based have been thoroughly researched. Documentation of such research can be found on page 62. While every possible effort has been made to ensure accuracy, the publisher will not assume liability for damages caused by inaccuracies in the data, and makes no warranty on the accuracy of the information contained herein.

Thanks to models Celeste Barry, Jake Beevers, Will Beevers, Danielle Boone, Dylan Boone, Abigail Lavold, Eli Robinson, Eve Robinson, Abigail Sandefur, Elena Seaholm, and Jessica Turner

**Library of Congress
Cataloging-in-Publication Data**
Boone, Mary.
 Midwestern recipes / by Mary Boone.
    p. cm. — (Kids can cook)
 Includes bibliographical references and index.
 ISBN 978-1-61228-071-4 (library bound)
 1. Cooking, American—Midwestern style. I. Title.
 TX715.2.M53B66 2012
 641.5977—dc23
                                            2011034448
eBook ISBN: 9781612281650

Printing   1   2   3   4   5   6   7   8   9

PLB

8838785

THE MENU

Located right smack in the middle of the United States is a region known as the Midwest. This part of the country is famous for its rich soil, long summers, and even longer winters.

The Midwest does not have exact geographic borders, and experts differ in their opinions about which states are truly Midwestern. What's certain is that the region runs across the north-central portion of the United States, and about 40 percent of the land within this area is dedicated to crop or livestock farming. For the purpose of this cookbook, we're focusing on the Midwestern states of Illinois, Indiana, Iowa, Michigan, Minnesota, Missouri, Ohio, and Wisconsin.

Also known as "America's breadbasket," the Midwest is a center for the United States' grain production, particularly wheat, corn, and soybeans. Beef and pork processing have long been important Midwestern industries. Chicago and Kansas City are known for their stockyard and processing centers, while Iowa remains king in terms of U.S. pork production.

Midwestern cooks traditionally shy away from bold, spicy flavors. Instead, they proudly serve dishes that showcase the abundance of locally grown foods.

Wisconsin is known as America's Dairyland, so it makes sense that milk and cheese are popular regional ingredients. The upper Midwest is a prime fruit-growing region: apples, blueberries, and cranberries can be found in abundance at the region's farmer's markets.

Immigrants from dozens of countries have made their homes in the Midwest—some of them arrived centuries ago, others more recently. These settlers have influenced the region's cuisine. Throughout the northern Midwest, for example, northern European immigrant groups brought recipes

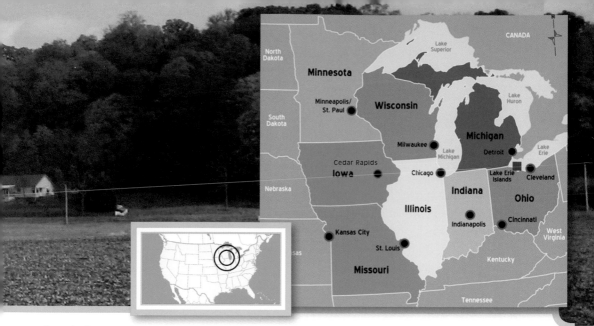

for dishes including Dutch and Swedish pancakes and Polish pierogi. The area's Native American influences are obvious in the widespread popularity of dishes featuring corn and wild rice.

The grueling work done by the region's farmers, miners, and railroad workers has helped shape Midwestern cuisine. Filling and inexpensive dishes were required to nourish these hardworking men and women. These requirements were met by the region's hot dishes (casseroles), pot roasts, potatoes, and gravy. They are the kinds of food your grandmother or great-grandmother might have made for Sunday dinner—but in the Midwest, they often appear on middle-of-the-week menus.

"People in the Midwest don't get complicated. They do very simple things," Chicago-based chef Stephen Langlois told Indiana's *Post-Tribune*. "But I say they do the simple things better than anyone else."

Within these pages you'll find a sampling of some very tasty recipes that have their roots in the Midwest. Whether you've ever visited Iowa or Illinois or Minnesota doesn't matter, because these dishes can help transport you to the Midwest and give you an idea of what Midwestern cuisine is all about.

Kitchen Safety

For successful cooking, be sure to read the recipe all the way through before you start. Assemble the ingredients and tools you'll need before you begin, and your projects will be much more fun.

Make certain your hair is tied back, your sleeves are rolled up for most cooking but down when frying, and your hands are washed. Wear oven mitts when handling anything hot. Stoves, ovens, and sharp items, such as knives and graters, should be used only under adult supervision.

Apple Pannekoeken

Pannekoeken (pronounced *pah-neh-KOO-ken*) are delicious Dutch pancakes that puff up in dramatic fashion and then deflate in the center to create a large edible bowl. There are savory pannekoeken, made with meats, vegetables, and cheeses; and sweet pannekoeken, topped with fruit, syrup, whipped cream, and even ice cream.

Sytje's Pannekoeken Huis Family Restaurants, a chain that at one time included 15 stores, was enormously popular in the 1980s and early 1990s and introduced thousands of Midwestern diners to these delectable Dutch pancakes. Many other Midwestern cafés have added pannekoeken—also known as Dutch babies—to their menus.

Pannekoeken pans are available in many cooking stores; if you don't have a special pan, you can bake this recipe in a pie tin or in an ovenproof skillet that has a rounded bottom. Try the topping recipe included here or, if you're rushed for time, top with warm pie filling.

Preparation time: 20 minutes
Cooking time: 15 to 18 minutes
Serves: 2

Ingredients

Pannekoeken
⅓ cup butter
3 large eggs
⅛ teaspoon salt
¾ cup milk
¾ cup flour

Topping
3 medium cooking apples
1 teaspoon cinnamon
¼ teaspoon nutmeg
⅛ teaspoon ground cloves
⅔ cup brown sugar
⅓ cup walnut pieces (optional)
⅓ cup butter
1 tablespoon flour

1. Place butter in an ovenproof pan with an 8- to 10-inch diameter.
2. Put the rack in the center of the oven; turn the oven on to 425°F.

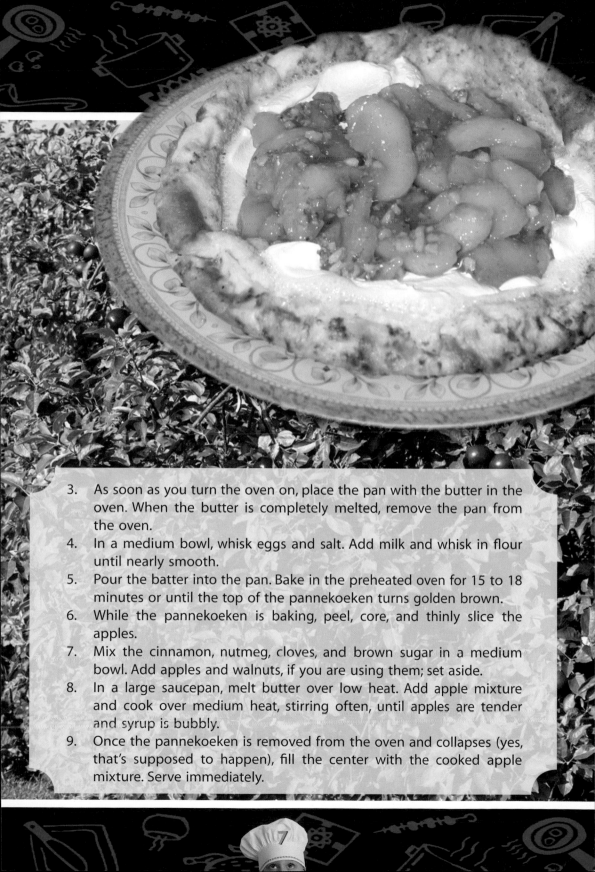

3. As soon as you turn the oven on, place the pan with the butter in the oven. When the butter is completely melted, remove the pan from the oven.

4. In a medium bowl, whisk eggs and salt. Add milk and whisk in flour until nearly smooth.

5. Pour the batter into the pan. Bake in the preheated oven for 15 to 18 minutes or until the top of the pannekoeken turns golden brown.

6. While the pannekoeken is baking, peel, core, and thinly slice the apples.

7. Mix the cinnamon, nutmeg, cloves, and brown sugar in a medium bowl. Add apples and walnuts, if you are using them; set aside.

8. In a large saucepan, melt butter over low heat. Add apple mixture and cook over medium heat, stirring often, until apples are tender and syrup is bubbly.

9. Once the pannekoeken is removed from the oven and collapses (yes, that's supposed to happen), fill the center with the cooked apple mixture. Serve immediately.

Kolaches

By the late 1850s, more than 10,000 Czechs had immigrated to the United States, many of them settling in Chicago. Large Czech communities were also established in or near St. Louis, Cleveland, Minneapolis, Milwaukee, and Cedar Rapids. Many of these communities celebrate their Czechoslovakian heritage with annual festivals—and many of those festivals pay homage to the kolache (pronounced *koh-LACH* or *koh-lah-SHAY*).

The kolache is a type of pastry consisting of fillings ranging from fruit or poppyseed to cheese or meat inside a golden bread nest. Originally a sweet Central European dessert, the pastries are also popular breakfast items.

Preparation time: 2 hours, 30 minutes (including rising time)
Cooking time: 8 to 10 minutes
Makes 30 to 36 kolaches

Ingredients

1 cup warm milk
1 envelope yeast
⅓ cup sugar, divided
⅓ cup butter, room temperature
  + 4 tablespoons butter
½ teaspoon salt

2 egg yolks
1 teaspoon grated lemon rind
3 cups flour
Jam, pie filling, or other filling of
  your choice

1. In small bowl, combine warm milk, yeast, and 1 tablespoon sugar. Set aside.
2. In a large mixing bowl and using an electric mixer, cream ⅓ cup butter, remaining sugar, and salt. Add egg yolks (you'll need to separate them from the whites), lemon rind, and yeast mixture.
3. Using a large wooden spoon, add flour ½ cup at a time, stirring as you go. When the dough gets too heavy to stir, mix with your hands. The dough should be glossy and sticky.
4. Make a dough ball and put it in an oiled mixing bowl, turning it to coat. Cover with waxed paper and place a clean kitchen towel over the waxed paper. Set the bowl in the refrigerator overnight.

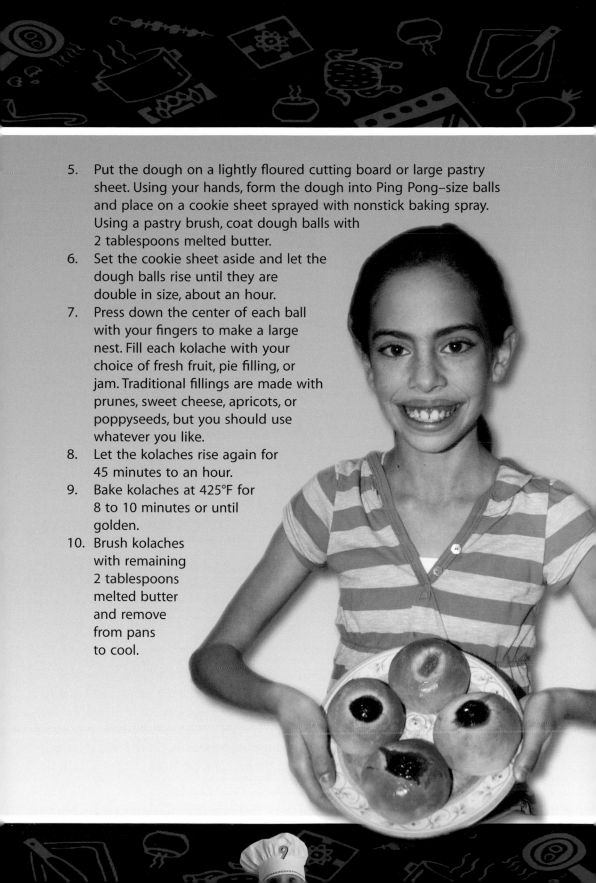

5. Put the dough on a lightly floured cutting board or large pastry sheet. Using your hands, form the dough into Ping Pong–size balls and place on a cookie sheet sprayed with nonstick baking spray. Using a pastry brush, coat dough balls with 2 tablespoons melted butter.

6. Set the cookie sheet aside and let the dough balls rise until they are double in size, about an hour.

7. Press down the center of each ball with your fingers to make a large nest. Fill each kolache with your choice of fresh fruit, pie filling, or jam. Traditional fillings are made with prunes, sweet cheese, apricots, or poppyseeds, but you should use whatever you like.

8. Let the kolaches rise again for 45 minutes to an hour.

9. Bake kolaches at 425°F for 8 to 10 minutes or until golden.

10. Brush kolaches with remaining 2 tablespoons melted butter and remove from pans to cool.

Easy Scrambled Eggs

Iowa farmers have more than 57 million laying hens that produce more than 14 billion eggs per year. That's a lot of omelets—especially when you consider that Iowa's neighboring states of Ohio, Indiana, and Minnesota are also among the nation's Top 10 egg producers.

One egg contains 6 grams of protein and some healthy unsaturated fats. Eggs are a good source of other nutrients as well, such as choline, which has been linked with preserving memory, and lutein and zeaxanthin, which may protect against vision loss. Egg yolks are in high cholesterol though, which can contribute to circulatory diseases, so many people limit the number of eggs they eat.

This easy egg recipe can be modified by adding diced ham, browned sausage, crumbled bacon, or cooked and diced vegetables. For quick cleanup, rinse your mixing bowl and utensils in cold water as soon as you are finished cooking. This will prevent the egg from hardening. Then, when you're ready to wash the dishes, be sure to use hot, soapy water.

Preparation time: 10 minutes
Cooking time: 5 minutes
Serves: 4 to 6

Ingredients

6 eggs
⅓ cup milk
¼ teaspoon salt
¼ teaspoon pepper
2 tablespoons butter or margarine

1. Break eggs into a medium-size bowl.
2. Add milk, salt, and pepper. Beat with a fork or wire whisk until foamy.
3. Place butter or margarine in a medium-size skillet. Place skillet on the stove over low heat.
4. When butter is melted, add beaten egg mixture. Slowly stir the eggs with a spatula, gently turning them, cooking until they are slightly firm.
5. Serve with toast and fresh fruit.

Apple Yogurt Salad

Michigan is the big player in the Midwest when it comes to apple production. The state's farmers routinely grow around 780 million pounds of apples per year. Orchards dot most states in the region, making apples a popular fall U-pick and farm stand product. Apples can be eaten fresh, baked into pies or cakes, or made into sauce or cider.

To get the most nutrition from an apple, you'll want to eat it with its skin on (which is what this salad recipe calls for). Almost half of an apple's vitamin C content is located just under the skin. Eating the skin also increases the amount of fiber you'll be getting. This nutrient helps move food through your digestive system. In some stores, apples are sold with a thin wax coating to make them look more appetizing, so be sure to wash them well.

There are hundreds of varieties of apples on the market. This recipe calls for Granny Smith apples, which are green, crisp, and tart. If you prefer a different type of apple, go ahead and make the substitution.

Preparation time: 10 minutes
Serves: 4

Ingredients

- 1 large or 2 medium Granny Smith apples
- 8 ounces fat-free vanilla yogurt
- 1 teaspoon chopped fresh mint
- 2 teaspoons honey
- 2 tablespoons granola

1. Wash, core, and chop the apple.
2. Combine yogurt, chopped apple, mint, and honey in a medium bowl.
3. Evenly divide apple-yogurt mixture between four bowls.
4. Just before serving, sprinkle each bowl with granola.

Honey Mustard Dressing

Beekeeping has been an important part of Midwest agriculture since the mid-1800s. In fact, a dispute over bees triggered the brief and bloodless Honey War between soldiers from Missouri and Iowa in the 1830s. A Missouri farmer started the dispute when he cut down three bee trees in land claimed by Iowa. The disagreement was ultimately settled by the United States Supreme Court.

Today, beekeepers take care of their bees in apiaries. They collect their honey and beeswax, or they produce bees for sale to other beekeepers. There are more than 300 varieties of honey found in the United States, and their flavor and color depend on the bees' nectar source. Nectar that comes from clover, for example, will produce honey that looks and tastes different than honey made from apple blossoms.

Whether you buy honey at the supermarket or at a local farmer's market, you can be assured it will add sweetness to everything from cakes and cookies to soups and, yes, even salad dressing.

Preparation time: 10 minutes
Serves: Makes 1¾ cups of dressing, enough for a dozen individual salads

Ingredients

1 cup mayonnaise
3 tablespoons orange juice
1 tablespoon half-and-half
4 tablespoons Dijon mustard
¼ cup honey
Salad vegetables of your choice

1. Combine everything but the salad vegetables in a bowl and mix well.
2. Make a green salad according to your family's tastes. Tear fresh, washed spinach or lettuce into bite-sized pieces. You may want to add green onions, tomatoes, nuts, crumbled bacon, or other ingredients.
3. Toss salad with dressing.
4. Leftover dressing can be stored covered in the refrigerator for up to 3 days.

Corn Fritters

Hot, humid Midwestern summers are perfect for growing sweet corn, which is one of the most popular vegetables in the region's home gardens, roadside stands, and farmer's markets.

Midwest sweet corn is available late summer through early fall. The starchy vegetable is at its best when it's boiled, roasted, or grilled and eaten right off the cob—brushed with butter, of course. Creative cooks, though, have long experimented with recipes for breads, salads, soups, and even desserts that feature sweet corn.

Most cooks don't set out to make corn fritters, which are like sweet biscuits. Rather, they're what happens when you cook too much corn-on-the-cob. With that in mind, the next time your family has sweet corn, you might want to toss a couple of extra ears into the kettle. These fritters are a very tasty treat, especially when served with tangy barbecued ribs or spicy chicken wings.

Preparation time: 10 minutes
Cooking time: 2 to 3 minutes per batch
Serves: 4 to 6

Ingredients

2 cups sweet corn, cooked and freshly cut from cobs	1/4 teaspoon salt
2 well-beaten eggs	2 tablespoons sugar
3 tablespoons flour	3 tablespoons butter
1/2 teaspoon baking powder	1 tablespoon oil
	Confectioners' sugar (optional)

1. Ask an adult to cut corn kernels from cobs (it will take two to three large ears of corn). To cut the kernels off a corn cob, place the flat, stem end in a bowl and run a serrated knife down the length of the ear using a sawing motion. The kernels will fall right into the bowl as they're cut off. (If no fresh corn is available, frozen will work.)
2. In a medium bowl, mix corn, eggs, flour, baking powder, salt, and sugar.

3. Melt butter and oil in a heavy skillet over medium heat. When melted, add batter by the heaping tablespoon. Let the fritters brown on one side, then flip them and let them brown on the other side. Don't overcook; you're shooting for a nice golden color.

4. Remove cooked fritters from the oil and drain them on a paper towel–lined plate. Keep fritters warm while you continue to cook the remaining batter.

5. Dust the fritters with powdered sugar if desired. Serve plain, buttered, or with pancake syrup or applesauce.

Toasted Ravioli

No one seems to know exactly where or when toasted ravioli was first served, but chefs on The Hill, a predominantly Italian neighborhood in St. Louis, claim it originated there. In fact, one of the most common tales revolves around a chef at Angelo's (a restaurant now known as Charlie Gitto's) who accidently dropped pasta into oil instead of water.

Regardless of the dish's origins, toasted ravioli has since become a regional favorite. *New York Times* reporter Patricia Brooks went so far as to write: "What spicy chicken wings are to Buffalo, toasted ravioli is to St. Louis." Several national restaurant chains have added toasted ravioli to their menus—most often as an appetizer—but it remains largely a Midwest specialty.

Of course, like most culinary creations, there are many variations on this recipe. Generally, some type of meat or cheese is wrapped in square ravioli, which is breaded then fried until the pasta becomes slightly crispy and golden brown. True Italian chefs often make their ravioli from scratch; this recipe relies on frozen, packaged ravioli, making it more easily and quickly prepared.

Preparation time: 10 minutes
Cooking time: 2 minutes per batch
Serves: 6

Ingredients

1   egg
2   tablespoons milk
¾   cup Italian seasoned breadcrumbs
½   teaspoon salt (optional)

½   of a 25-ounce package of frozen cheese ravioli, thawed
3   cups vegetable oil
1   tablespoon Parmesan cheese
16-ounce jar marinara sauce

1.   Whisk egg and milk in a small bowl.
2.   Place breadcrumbs and, if desired, salt in a shallow bowl.
3.   Dip ravioli in milk mixture and then in breadcrumbs, turning to coat both sides.
4.   In a saucepan, heat marinara sauce over medium heat until bubbling. Reduce heat to simmer.

5. In a large, heavy pan, pour vegetable oil to a depth of two inches; heat oil over medium to high heat. You'll know the oil is hot enough when you drop a small amount of breading into it and it sizzles and turns brown.
6. Fry ravioli, a few at a time, for one minute on each side or until golden.
7. Drain ravioli on paper towels. Sprinkle with Parmesan cheese.
8. Serve immediately with marinara sauce for dipping.

Wild Rice Soup

Wild rice can be found in many parts of the United States, where it is sometimes known as Canada rice, Indian rice, manoomin, or water oats. Minnesota contributes about half of the nation's production of this grain.

In the past, natural stands of wild rice provided a staple in the diets of local Native American groups. Today, this flavorful grain is cultivated primarily in the north-central portion of the state.

Virtually all wild rice is grown in flooded fields. The soil needs to be saturated from the time the seeds germinate in the spring until two to three weeks before harvest. Wild rice is actually an annual grass. Known for its nutty flavor and dark color, wild rice is high in protein and easy to prepare. This soup is simple to make and tastes great on a cold winter night.

Preparation time: 25 minutes
Cooking Time: 30 minutes
Serves: 4 to 6

Ingredients

3 tablespoons butter	Salt and pepper to taste
½ medium onion, diced	2 cups milk
1 medium carrot, diced	1 cup cubed, cooked chicken
1 stalk celery, chopped	1 cup cooked wild rice
3 tablespoons flour	10.5-ounce can chicken broth

1. Melt butter in a large saucepan.
2. Sauté onions, carrots, and celery in butter until tender but not crisp.
3. Add flour, salt, and pepper to vegetable mixture; stir.
4. Add milk and chicken broth; stir until thickened.
5. Stir in rice and chicken; heat through. Serve as a first course or as a hearty main dish.

Wisconsin Cheese Soup

Wisconsin is the nation's top cheese-producing state. Wisconsin cheese-makers may be best known for their cheddar and Colby, but there are actually more than 600 varieties, styles, and types of cheese produced there.

It makes sense, then, that cheese is a featured ingredient in many Midwestern dishes. And what better way to beat the region's subzero winter temperatures than with a bowl of steaming hot Wisconsin cheese soup?

A rich and creamy blend of vegetables and cheese, this basic soup recipe can be altered according to your personal tastes and the ingredients you have on hand. Sliced mushrooms, diced celery or potatoes, leftover ham or sausage—all make great add-ins. You can also experiment with different cheeses. Instead of 2 cups of cheddar, for example, you might try blending a cup of cheddar with a cup of Gouda, Swiss, or even pepper jack.

Preparation time: 15 minutes
Cooking time: 20 minutes
Serves: 4 to 6

Ingredients

- 1 cup sliced carrots
- 2 cups chopped broccoli
- 1 cup water
- 1 teaspoon chicken bouillon granules
- ¼ cup chopped onion
- ¼ cup butter
- ¼ cup flour
- ¼ teaspoon ground black pepper
- 2 cups milk
- 2 cups + ¼ cup shredded sharp cheddar cheese
- Salt and pepper to taste
- 2 tablespoons fresh chives, chopped

1. In a small saucepan, over medium heat, combine carrots, broccoli, water, and bouillon. Bring to a boil. Reduce heat, cover and simmer for five minutes.
2. Remove from heat and set aside.
3. In a large saucepan, cook onion in butter over medium heat until onion is tender and translucent.
4. Add flour and pepper to onion mixture. Stir and cook one minute.
5. Add milk to onion mixture. Stir and bring to a boil. Reduce heat, add 2 cups cheese, and stir until cheese is melted. To avoid curdling, do not allow the soup to boil after cheese is added.
6. Stir in reserved vegetables and cooking liquid. Salt and pepper to taste; heat through.
7. Ladle soup into bowls and garnish with a sprinkle of fresh chives and grated cheese before serving.

Chicago Deep-Dish Pizza

New Yorkers have their thin crust. Californians have their unique toppings (think goat cheese, avocados, and eggs). And Chicagoans have their deep-dish pizza.

Chicago-style pizza, developed in the 1940s, has a buttery crust up to three inches tall at the edge. This super-filling pizza is also loaded with larger-than-normal amounts of cheese and chunky tomato sauce.

Visitors flock to the pizza places that made this style of pizza famous: Pizzeria Uno and Due, Gino's Pizza, Giordano's, and Lou Malnati's are among some of the most popular. Many of these shops sell and ship their pizza pies to fans who can't find the thick-crust version where they live.

Most Chicago pizzerias also serve thin-crust pizza, but the term *Chicago-style pizza* is used to describe this deep-dish style of pizza.

Preparation time: 4 hours 30 minutes, including rising time
Cooking time: 40 minutes
Makes two 10-inch pizzas

Ingredients

Dough
2 cups warm (not hot) water
1 teaspoon rapid-rise, dry yeast
¾ teaspoon salt
¼ cup olive oil
5 ½ cups flour
2 tablespoons cornmeal

Toppings
2 cups chunky tomato sauce, homemade or in a jar
2 cups shredded mozzarella
Plus your choice of any combination of topping such as the following:
½ cup sliced mushrooms ½ cup sliced pepperoni
½ cup spinach, shredded ½ cup browned Italian sausage
½ cup grated Romano   ½ cup grated Parmesan

1. In the bowl of a stand-style mixer, combine water and yeast. Allow yeast to dissolve.
2. Add salt, olive oil, and flour. Using a dough hook attachment, mix dough on low speed. Once a ball has formed, mix on medium speed for another 1 to 2 minutes, until dough becomes elastic and smooth. (This process can be done by hand kneading, but beware: the dough is very stiff.)
3. Allow the dough to rise for 2 to 4 hours. Once it has risen, divide dough in half and dust each ball with flour.
4. Preheat oven to 425°F.
5. Prepare two 10-inch round deep-dish pizza pans or baking dishes. Grease the pans using olive oil or butter; spread evenly on bottom and sides of pan using your fingers or a folded paper towel. Sprinkle one tablespoon of cornmeal on the bottom of each pan.
6. Place a dough ball in each pan. Using your fingers, spread dough along the bottom of the pan and at least one inch up the sides.
7. Top dough with sauce, mozzarella, and toppings of your choice.
8. Bake pizza for 30 to 40 minutes, until golden.
9. Let the pizza rest 5 minutes so that the cheese sets, then serve.

Horseshoe Sandwich

The horseshoe sandwich was first served in the late 1920s by chef Joe Schweska at the Leland Hotel in Springfield, Illinois; it's been a local favorite ever since. The first horseshoe was made from ham cut from the bone in the shape of a horseshoe and placed on top of two thick slices of toast. A sauce made of sharp white cheddar cheese was poured over the meat, and fried potato wedges were placed on top.

Today, the horseshoe is made dozens of different ways. Almost all recipes start with the toast or bread on the bottom. Meat comes next. Hamburger patties and ham are most commonly featured; other popular meats include sliced turkey, roast beef, chicken, or fried fish. The meat is covered in french fries, and cheese sauce covers the whole dish.

Restaurant-style horseshoes are typically huge, covering an entire dinner plate or platter. Many menus offer "pony" or half-sized versions of the famous sandwich.

This recipe is made with ground beef. You can substitute another meat if you prefer.

Preparation time: 40 minutes
Cooking time: 25 minutes
Serves: 6

Ingredients

28-ounce package frozen french fries (or homemade)
1½ pounds ground beef
6 slices Texas toast or other thick bread
¼ cup butter
½ cup flour

4 cups milk
12-ounce can evaporated milk
½ pound sharp cheddar cheese
2 to 3 teaspoons Worcestershire sauce
2 to 3 dashes hot sauce
Salt and pepper to taste

1. Preheat oven to 400°F.
2. Place fries in a large, resealable plastic bag and spray thoroughly with cooking spray. Shake the bag to distribute the oil.
3. Place fries on a large baking sheet. Bake for 20 minutes or until golden and sizzling.
4. While fries are cooking, form ground beef into six thin patties.
5. Cook patties in a large frying pan over medium to high heat. Cook 2 to 3 minutes per side; season to taste. Keep patties warm while constructing the sandwich.
6. To make the sauce: Melt butter over medium heat in a heavy saucepan; stir in flour. Cook and continue to stir until mixture thickens (3 to 5 minutes).
7. Gradually stir in the four cups of milk. Stir and cook until the mixture thickens again.
8. Whisk in evaporated milk. Add cheddar and continue to stir until cheese melts. Add Worcestershire and hot pepper sauce to taste.
9. Toast bread until crisp. Slice diagonally.
10. Place two bread triangles on each of six plates. Place one ground beef patty atop the bread on each plate. Divide half the fries among the six plates, covering the meat and bread. Top fries with a large serving of cheese sauce. Divide the other half of the fries among the six plates, adding them to the top of each cheesy mountain.
11. Use a knife and fork to eat this gooey goodness. Make certain you have plenty of napkins available.

Just Like Maid-Rites™

In Muscatine, Iowa, a butcher named Fred Angell was experimenting with recipes back in 1926 when he came up with a tasty sandwich that launched one of the nation's first restaurant chains: Maid-Rite™.

Maid-Rite™ restaurants are prevalent throughout the Midwest; the franchise has a more limited presence in the southern and western United States. Traditional Maid-Rites™ (also known as loose meat sandwiches) are served with pickles and mustard only—no ketchup!

The recipe for the restaurant version of this famous sandwich is a well-guarded secret. Many Midwestern cooks, though, have created taste-alike versions of the famous Maid-Rite™ sandwich. Try this recipe for a sandwich that's both simple and filling.

Preparation time: 10 minutes
Cooking time: 35 minutes
Serves: 10

Ingredients

1½ pounds lean ground beef
1 medium onion, minced
1 tablespoon prepared mustard
½ cup water
1 tablespoon Worcestershire sauce
¼ teaspoon salt (or to taste)
10 hamburger buns

1. Place ground beef and onion in a medium-sized saucepan. Cook over low to medium heat for 8 to 10 minutes; use a spoon to break up meat and continue to stir until all the pink has disappeared and the meat has turned brown. Drain fat.
2. Add mustard, water, Worcestershire sauce, and salt. When the liquid comes to a boil, reduce heat. Simmer for 20 minutes.
3. Use a large slotted spoon to scoop meat mixture onto warmed buns.

Pork Tenderloin Sandwich

Breaded tenderloin sandwiches are a fixture on the menus of diners and cafés throughout the Midwest. Filmmaker Jensen Rufe made a 1998 documentary about the beloved sandwich: *In Search of the Famous Hoosier Breaded Pork Tenderloin Sandwich*, and the Iowa Pork Producers Association annually honors that state's best breaded tenderloin (310 restaurants were nominated in 2010).

The tenderloin sandwich contains a breaded and fried pork cutlet similar to wiener schnitzel. The *tender* in *tenderloin* refers to the ease with which you can sink your teeth into it. You start with a boneless loin that you tenderize with a meat mallet.

It's a tradition in many Midwest restaurants to serve a dinner-plate-sized tenderloin on a regular-sized bun, with three-quarters of the meat going bunless. Diners can ask for an extra bun, cut the loin in half and stack it on the bun or—more likely—ask for a doggie bag, so that the rest of the loin can be eaten in a second sandwich the next day.

Preparation time: 25 minutes
Cooking time: 4 minutes per tenderloin slice
Serves: 4

Ingredients

- 1 pound boneless pork loin, cut into 1-inch slices
- 1 cup whole milk
- 1 egg
- 24–36 saltine crackers, pulverized into crumbs (a food processor works great)
- $\frac{1}{2}$ teaspoon ground black pepper
- Vegetable oil or solid vegetable shortening
- 4 sandwich buns

1. When you buy your pork loin, ask your butcher to trim the fat and cut it into 1-inch slices (another adult can also do this for you).

2. Place each slice between two pieces of waxed paper or plastic wrap. Using the flat side of a meat mallet, beat the loin slices until they are much larger in diameter and about $\frac{1}{4}$ inch thick.
3. Whisk together the egg and milk in a shallow bowl.
4. In another shallow bowl, mix cracker crumbs and pepper.
5. Dip each slice of pork into the milk mixture and then into the crackers, pressing down to ensure the loin is well coated with crumbs. Set the coated tenderloins aside to set up for a few moments while you prepare the oil. This will help the crumbs stick to the meat; do not stack the slices.
6. In a large, heavy skillet, heat $\frac{1}{2}$ inch of shortening or cooking oil until it sizzles when a pinch of breadcrumbs is dropped in.
7. Fry the tenderloins, one or two at a time, for $1\frac{1}{2}$ to 2 minutes per side, turning once.
8. Keep tenderloins warm in a low-temperature oven while you cook the remaining slices.
9. Serve tenderloins warm on buns with your choice of condiments.

Tater Tots™ Hot Dish

Casseroles are popular throughout the Midwest. They are easy-to-make, one-dish meals that are warm and filling—perfect for cold, snowy days. Because they're inexpensive and easy to reheat, the dishes are well suited for large family meals, feeding seasonal farm crews, or taking to church dinners.

In the upper Midwest—most notably in Minnesota—these tasty casseroles are known as hot dishes. There are many variations on the hot dish, but they almost always contain a protein (turkey, ground beef, tuna, beans), a starch (noodles, potatoes), and a vegetable (green beans, carrots, peas); cheese, canned soups, and onion crisps are also popular ingredients.

Dozens of cookbooks are devoted to hot dish recipes and many regional restaurants feature the dishes on their menus. While every cook may add his or her own special ingredients, this recipe represents a true regional favorite.

Preparation time: 20 minutes
Cooking time: 45 to 60 minutes
Serves: 8 to 10

Ingredients

1½ pounds ground beef
½ medium onion, diced
15-ounce can green beans (or substitute 1¾ cup fresh green beans that have been washed, trimmed, and cut into 1-inch pieces)

10.75-ounce can cream of mushroom soup, concentrated
10.75-ounce can cream of celery soup, concentrated
32-ounce package Tater Tots™ frozen shredded potatoes
Salt and pepper to taste

1. Preheat oven to 350°F.
2. Prepare a 9 x 13-inch baking dish by spraying it with nonstick cooking spray.
3. Heat a medium-sized skillet over medium to high heat for a couple minutes. Add ground beef to the pan. Stir and turn the meat so that it breaks up as it cooks. After 2 minutes of cooking, add onion to the skillet. Continue to stir until all the pink has disappeared and the meat has browned (5 to 7 minutes).
4. Using a slotted spoon, transfer ground beef and onion mixture to the bottom of the baking dish.
5. Drain green beans and place them in an even layer over the ground beef.
6. In a small bowl, mix the two cans of soup (do not dilute with milk or water). Spread the combined soups over the base layer of the hot dish.
7. Top evenly with Tater Tots™ potatoes. Season with salt and pepper if desired.
8. Bake uncovered for 45 minutes to 1 hour, or until brown and bubbly.
9. Scoop onto plates. Serve with a fresh salad.

City "Chicken"

Today, chicken is an affordable dish, but in the early 1900s, it was too expensive for most people to buy and serve. To mimic the fancy fried chicken feasts enjoyed by the wealthy, creative cooks came up with a mock version called City Chicken. Instead of chicken, this recipe uses cubed pork, which was more affordable at the time. Other versions of this recipe rely on cubed veal or ground pork or beef. Arranging the meat on skewers made each serving look like a chicken leg and let people pretend they were eating the real thing.

Preparation time: 20 minutes
Cooking time: 30 minutes
Serves: 4

Ingredients

1 pound lean pork cut into 1-inch cubes
1 cup seasoned breadcrumbs
1 egg
⅓ cup milk
6 short wooden skewers
Oil for frying

1. Soak 8 to 10 wooden skewers in a bowl of water for about 10 minutes (this keeps the skewers from catching on fire while cooking).
2. Preheat oven to 350°F.
3. Mix egg and milk together; set aside.
4. Put breadcrumbs in a pie plate or cake pan; set aside.
5. Thread pork onto skewers. Skewer the cubes through one corner, alternating the side of the skewer the meat is on to create the look of a drumstick.
6. Dip the kabobs into the egg mixture, then roll in breadcrumbs until coated.
7. In a large skillet, heat butter and oil over medium heat. Brown kabobs until golden brown, turning frequently (5 to 8 minutes).
8. Remove kabobs from skillet and place onto a baking sheet. Bake for 15 or 20 minutes, until juices run clear.

Turkey Cucumber Dill Sandwiches

Want to talk turkey? Look no further than the Midwest.

Minnesota is the number one turkey producing and processing state in the United States, with 250 family farmers raising approximately 49 million turkeys annually. Missouri, Indiana, and Iowa also are among the nation's top turkey-producing states. Turkey is a high-protein, low-fat menu choice that's naturally low in cholesterol. It's delicious roasted, barbecued, and even deep-fried.

According to the National Turkey Federation, more than 25 percent of U.S. households consume turkey deli meat at least once every two weeks. Try this easy recipe to add zest to your regular turkey sandwich.

Preparation time: 10 minutes
Serves: 4

Ingredients

- 1/4 cup mayonnaise
- 1 tablespoon dried dill weed
- 8 slices multigrain bread or mini rolls
- 1/2 pound sliced cooked deli turkey (or use thin-sliced fresh turkey)
- Sprig of dill
- 4 slices dill Havarti or Muenster cheese
- 16 thin slices cucumber
- 4 lettuce leaves (optional)

1. Mix mayonnaise and dill in a small bowl.
2. Spread mayonnaise mixture onto one side of each bread slice.
3. Top these with turkey, cheese, cucumber, and lettuce, if desired. Top with remaining bread.
4. Cut each sandwich in quarters and use a toothpick in each section to hold the layers together. (You do not need to do this if you are using mini rolls.)
5. Remove toothpicks before eating. Serve with carrot and celery sticks.

Baked Apples

Most apples in the United States are eaten fresh, but they're also tasty in pies, cakes, muffins, and more. Baked apples are popular in North America and beyond. *Bratapfel* is German for "baked apple," where it is a much-loved Christmas dessert. In England, baked apples are considered traditional English "puddings" (desserts) and are often filled with jam or mincemeat.

Generally, baked apples are made with cooking-style apples such as Braeburn, Cortland, Fuji, Gala, or Granny Smith. The truth is, any apple will do. Size, though, is important, because you'll want plenty of room to hold your sweet stuffing.

Let this recipe guide your cooking adventure and then add or subtract ingredients according to your tastes. **Hint:** Raisins, pecans, and caramel would be terrific ingredients with which to experiment!

Ingredients

Butter or cooking spray
4 large apples
¼ cup wheat germ
¼ cup dried cherries, cut into pieces
3 tablespoons chopped walnuts
1 tablespoon fresh lemon juice
¼ teaspoon cinnamon

¼ teaspoon nutmeg
1 tablespoon brown sugar
⅛ teaspoon salt
1 tablespoon flour
¾ cup apple juice
Whipped cream or ice cream
  (optional)

1. Preheat oven to 350°F.
2. Prepare a shallow baking dish with nonstick cooking spray or by coating bottom and sides with softened butter or margarine.
3. With an adult's help, core the apples without going all the way through (you're making a well in the apple that you're going to fill). Peel the apples about halfway down and then place them, opening-side up, in the baking dish.
4. In a small bowl, combine wheat germ, dried cherries, nuts, lemon juice, cinnamon, nutmeg, sugar and salt.

5. Fill the hollow portion of each apple with the wheat germ mixture.
6. Mix the flour and apple juice in a small bowl. Pour a little of this mixture over each of the apples.
7. Bake 40 minutes or until the apple is tender enough to be easily pierced. You can eat the apples just like this, or serve them with whipped cream or ice cream.

Caramel Corn

In 1492, Christopher Columbus received a gift of popcorn from Native Americans who greeted him and his crew. At the first Thanksgiving, in 1621, the Wampanoag Indians brought bowls full of popcorn to the meal. And, in the 1700s, colonial women began making an early version of breakfast cereal by pouring milk and sugar over popped corn.

Today, the average American eats a whopping 68 quarts of popcorn each year—most of it grown in the Midwest. With miles and miles of cornfields, it's not surprising that Illinois, Indiana, Iowa, Kansas, Michigan, Missouri, Nebraska, and Ohio are among the world's top popcorn-producing areas. Popcorn resembles corn-on-the-cob in appearance and cultivation. Popcorn kernels, though, are the only ones with the ability to pop.

Popcorn on its own is a terrific snack, but when you're aching for something sweet, this caramel corn is hard to resist.

Preparation time: 15 minutes
Cooking time: 60 minutes
Makes 5 quarts

Ingredients

- 5 quarts popped popcorn
- 1 cup butter
- 2 cups brown sugar
- 1/2 cup corn syrup
- 1 teaspoon salt
- 1/2 teaspoon baking soda
- 1 teaspoon vanilla extract

1. Preheat oven to 250°F.
2. Place popped popcorn in a very large bowl.
3. In a medium saucepan, over medium heat, melt butter. Stir in brown sugar, corn syrup, and salt. Bring to a boil, stirring constantly. Once the mixture begins to bubble, stop stirring and let it continue to boil for 4 minutes.

4. Remove saucepan from heat and stir in baking soda and vanilla.
5. Pour the sauce in a thin stream over popcorn, stirring quickly to coat all kernels.
6. Place popcorn on two large cookie sheets and bake for one hour, stirring every 15 minutes.
7. Remove from oven and cool completely before breaking into pieces.

Frozen Vanilla Custard

Frozen custard is a creamy, rich gourmet dessert. It was first introduced as an East Coast carnival treat in the early 1900s. In 1933, the delicacy was served at the World's Fair in Chicago. Midwesterners almost immediately embraced the dessert as their own. Frozen custard became—and has remained—a popular treat in towns ranging from Milwaukee to St. Louis and Kansas City to Lafayette, Indiana.

What makes frozen custard different from ice cream? In the United States, frozen custard must contain at least 10 percent butterfat and 1.4 percent egg yolks. If it contains less egg yolk, the dessert is considered ice cream—not custard. Commercially produced custards are made with special machines that are designed to remove the air that's typically whipped into ice cream. Less air and fewer ice crystals result in a dessert that's silky smooth.

While home cooks don't have access to specialized production equipment, this recipe will help you create a similar-tasting treat.

Preparation Time: 2 hours 30 minutes, including freezer time
Cooking time: 10 minutes
Serves: 8

Ingredients

3 eggs, beaten
⅔ cup sugar
1 cup half-and-half cream
1 cup whipping cream

1 teaspoon vanilla extract
¼ teaspoon salt
Toppings of choice (optional)

1. Beat eggs and sugar in a medium mixing bowl and set aside.
2. In a heavy saucepan and using a cooking thermometer, heat half-and-half to 160 degrees; stir occasionally, being careful not to scald it.
3. When half-and-half reaches the appropriate temperature, slowly pour half of it into the egg mixture, stirring as you pour. Stir well, then add the remaining cream to the egg mixture.

4. Place the egg and half-and-half mixture back into the heavy saucepan and cook over low to medium heat; heat, stirring constantly, until thickened.
5. Remove mixture from burner and set aside to cool for 5 to 10 minutes.
6. Pour egg and cream mixture into a shallow cake pan and place in a level spot in the freezer, freezing to a mushy consistency (do not freeze hard).
7. Using a mixer, whip cream; add vanilla and salt. Continue whipping until stiff peaks form in the cream.
8. Fold whipped cream into partially frozen mixture. Return to pan and freeze at least one hour.
9. Serve frozen custard plain, or add a topping such as chocolate syrup or fresh fruit.

Iowa Chocolate Cake

"The Open Line" was a popular cooking radio show based in Cedar Rapids, Iowa, for more than 40 years. The show issued several cookbooks showcasing listeners' recipes. This recipe for Iowa Chocolate Cake is included in several of those cookbooks and was the show's first "most requested recipe" back in 1963.

The cake has made its way to many 4-H fairs, family potlucks, and birthday celebrations for three primary reasons: it's simple to make, it's incredibly moist, and it's delicious.

Preparation time: 20 minutes + time to cool before frosting
Cooking time: 45 minutes
Makes one 9 x 13-inch cake, 20 to 24 pieces of cake

Ingredients

Cake

¾ cup shortening +
    1 tablespoon to prepare pan
2 cups sugar
1½ cups boiling water
2 cups all-purpose flour +
    1 tablespoon to prepare pan

2 teaspoons baking soda
½ cup unsweetened baking cocoa
    + 1 tablespoon to prepare pan
½ teaspoon salt
2 eggs, beaten
1 teaspoon vanilla

1. Preheat oven to 350°F.
2. Prepare a 9 x 13-inch pan by coating bottom and sides with 1 tablespoon shortening. Then sprinkle 1 tablespoon of flour and 1 tablespoon of cocoa inside the pan. Shake it to coat all surfaces with a light dusting. Turn the pan upside down over the sink to tap out the excess.
3. Put the shortening and sugar in a mixing bowl and cover with boiling water. Stir to mix.
4. Sift flour, baking soda, cocoa, and salt and add to hot mixture. Stir. You can use an electric mixer, but the batter is so thin that a wooden spoon will do just fine.

5. Add eggs and vanilla; stir well.
6. Pour the batter into prepared pan. Remember, the batter will be thin.
7. Bake 35 to 45 minutes or until the cake pulls away from the sides of the pan.
8. Let it cool completely. You can make your own frosting to go with it—the recipe is included—or you can rely on a can of purchased frosting.

Frosting
2 tablespoons melted butter
   or margarine
3 tablespoons milk
1 tablespoon baking cocoa
2 cups confectioners' sugar

To make the frosting, mix butter, milk, and cocoa in small bowl with electric mixer. Add one cup confectioners' sugar and mix. Continue to add confectioners' sugar one tablespoon at a time until you reach the consistency you desire (you may not need the whole two cups).

Strawberry Shortcake

Rich, ripe strawberries are the stars of Midwest gardens and farmer's markets each June and July. The deep red color and simple sweetness of a strawberry can brighten up both the taste and appearance of any meal. Is it any wonder strawberries are the most popular berry in the world?

Strawberries are delicious in pies, muffins, and salads. But no dish showcases the strawberry's juicy goodness like an old-fashioned strawberry shortcake. Strawberry shortcake consists of a white cake or biscuit topped with sliced strawberries (fresh are best) and whipped cream.

You can buy pre-baked cakes that make assembling this dessert even simpler, but there really is nothing like a fresh-baked biscuit. Here's an excellent recipe for strawberry shortcake that features tasty made-from-scratch biscuits.

Preparation time: 25 minutes
Cooking time: 20 minutes
Serves: 8

Ingredients

- 6 cups strawberries, rinsed, hulled and quartered
- 1¼ cups plus 2 tablespoons sugar
- 3 cups all-purpose flour
- 4 teaspoons baking powder
- ¾ teaspoon salt
- 12 tablespoons cold unsalted butter cut into small pieces
- 2 cups heavy cream, divided
- 2 large eggs
- ½ teaspoon vanilla

1. Preheat oven to 375°F.
2. In a medium bowl, toss strawberries with ¾ cup sugar; let sit to bring out their juices.
3. In a food processor, pulse flour, baking powder, ½ cup sugar, and the salt until combined.
4. Add butter to food processor bowl and pulse until mixture resembles coarse meal but with some pea-size bits of butter remaining.
5. In a medium bowl, whisk together ½ cup cream and eggs.

TIP: You can dip the strawberries in melted chocolate before adding them to the shortcake.

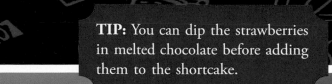

6. Pour cream mixture into food processor bowl over flour mixture; pulse until some large clumps begin to form.
7. Using a half-cup measuring cup, gently pack dough, invert, and then tap out onto a prepared baking sheet. Repeat to form 8 biscuits. Bake until lightly golden, about 20 minutes. Transfer to a rack to cool, about 15 minutes.
8. Using an electric mixer, beat remaining 1½ cups cream and 2 tablespoons sugar with the vanilla until soft peaks form.
9. When the biscuits have cooled, slice them in half horizontally. Spoon strawberries and their liquid over bottom halves. Spoon whipped cream over strawberries, and replace top halves of biscuits.

Sunny Sunflower Cookies

Native to the fertile Great Plains, sunflowers grow naturally under the hot Midwestern sun. Native Americans cultivated and enjoyed the sunflower, using the nutty-tasting seed kernels for a quick energy boost. Sunflower seeds are rich in protein, fiber, iron, and vitamin E; the fat in sunflower seeds is polyunsaturated, so they contain no cholesterol. Today, commercially available sunflower seeds are easy to use, rich in flavor, and perfect for salads, desserts, entrées, snacks, and baked goods. When it comes to baking, you'll want to buy sunflower kernels, which means the hulls have already been mechanically removed.

Preparation time: 20 minutes
Cooking time: 8 to 10 minutes per batch
Makes 48 cookies

Ingredients

1 cup margarine
2 eggs
1 cup granulated sugar
1 cup brown sugar, packed
1 teaspoon vanilla
2 cups flour
1 teaspoon baking soda

$^1/_2$ teaspoon baking powder
$^1/_4$ teaspoon salt
2 cups rolled oats
1 cup coconut, flaked
1 cup raw or roasted sunflower
    kernels

1. Preheat oven to 400°F.
2. In a medium bowl, combine margarine, eggs, and sugars until well blended. Add vanilla and blend again.
3. Add flour, baking soda, baking powder, and salt to margarine mixture. Mix well.
4. Stir in oats, coconut, and sunflower kernels.
5. Drop by rounded tablespoons onto an ungreased baking sheet.
6. Bake 8 to 10 minutes or until cookies are light brown around the edges. Cool on a rack.

Christmas Tree-shaped Cheese Ball

What would a Midwestern holiday be without cheese? This tasty cheese ball—which isn't a ball at all—is bound to be a hit with your holiday guests. With a little creativity, you can transform the traditional cheese ball into a tree shape. We suggest decorating with pine nuts and chopped pimiento, but if those ingredients don't suit your tastes, do some experimenting. Perhaps you'll want to make your "ornaments" out of diced red and yellow peppers, or maybe you'd prefer a "garland" made of sliced almonds. Whether your holiday gathering is fancy or family-oriented, partygoers are sure to love this appetizer, which tastes as good as it looks.

Preparation Time: 30 minutes + 4 hours in refrigerator
Makes 7 cups cheese spread

Ingredients

12 ounces cream cheese, softened
2 cups shredded Cheddar cheese (16 ounces)
1 tablespoon basil pesto
1 tablespoon grated onion
¼ cup finely chopped parsley
¼ cup toasted pine nuts
2 tablespoons jarred pimiento, chopped
Slice of cheddar or other firm cheese of your choice
Assorted crackers

1. Mix together cream cheese and cheddar cheese.
2. Stir pesto and grated onion into the cheese mixture.
3. Cover the cheese with plastic wrap and refrigerate at least four hours or until firm enough to shape.
4. Place the cheese mixture on a cookie sheet. Shape the cheese into a cone to look like a pine tree. You can either wrap and freeze the tree at this point, or continue to prepare it. The tree can be frozen for up to one month. Twelve hours before serving, remove tree from freezer. Thaw in plastic wrap in refrigerator.
5. Before serving, roll the tree in chopped parsley, pressing it evenly onto the tree. Press pine nuts onto the tree to form a garland. Press chopped pimiento onto the tree for ornaments. Top the tree with a star cut from cheddar cheese.
6. Serve with crackers.

Cranberry Appetizer Meatballs

The cranberry is one of North America's few native fruits (some others are the blueberry and Concord grape). Cranberries were first used by Native Americans, who discovered the berry's versatility as a food, fabric dye, and healing agent. Today, cranberries are commercially grown throughout the northern part of the United States, including in Wisconsin and Michigan.

This recipe starts with homemade meatballs. If you're short of time, buy frozen, premade meatballs, which you can heat according to package instructions, then top with this tasty sauce.

Preparation time: 35 minutes
Cooking time: 45 minutes
Makes 84 meatballs

Ingredients

Meatballs
- 2 eggs, lightly beaten
- 1 cup dry breadcrumbs
- ½ cup minced fresh parsley
- ⅓ cup ketchup
- 2 tablespoons finely chopped onion
- 2 tablespoons soy sauce
- 2 garlic cloves, minced
- ½ teaspoon salt
- ¼ teaspoon pepper
- 2 pounds lean ground beef

Cranberry Sauce
- 14-ounce can whole-berry cranberry sauce
- 12-ounce bottle chili sauce
- 1 tablespoon brown sugar
- 1 tablespoon prepared mustard
- 1 tablespoon lemon juice

1. Preheat oven to 400°F.
2. Combine eggs, breadcrumbs, parsley, ketchup, onion, soy sauce, garlic, salt, and pepper in a bowl.
3. Crumble beef over mixture; use hands to combine.
4. Shape meat into one-inch balls.
5. Place meatballs on a shallow baking tray. Bake uncovered for 15 minutes or until no longer pink inside.

6. While meatballs are cooking, combine cranberry sauce, chili sauce, brown sugar, mustard, and lemon juice in a saucepan. Cook over medium heat, stirring until smooth.
7. Using a slotted spoon, transfer cooked meatballs to a slow cooker or chafing dish, and pour sauce over meatballs.
8. Serve warm.

Independence Day Cranberry Chiller

Wisconsin farmers grow more than half the cranberries raised in the United States. The fruit contributes nearly $350 million annually to the state's economy and supports more than 7,200 jobs across the state.

Cranberries are grown on low-trailing vines in sandy or peat marshes. In Wisconsin, those marshes are flooded with water to aid in harvesting. Because the berries contain a pocket of air, when the marshes are flooded, the berries float to the surface, where they are picked up by harvesting equipment.

The tart cranberry is very versatile, making its way into everything from salads and breads to trail mix and cookies. This tasty drink recipe will quench thirsts any day of the year, but its pretty red coloring makes it a perfect Fourth of July beverage.

Preparation time: 10 minutes
Serves: 12 to 14

Ingredients

1 quart cranberry juice, room
   temperature
¼ cup sugar
6-ounce can frozen lemonade
   concentrate, undiluted
6-ounce can frozen limeade
   concentrate, undiluted
1 liter club soda, chilled

1. In large pitcher or punch bowl, combine cranberry juice and sugar. Stir to dissolve sugar.
2. Add frozen lemonade and limeade concentrates. Stir until melted.
3. Just before serving, add club soda. Stir.
4. Serve in tall glasses with ice cubes.

Potato Latkes

Latkes are pan-fried pancakes made of grated potato, flour, and egg; many recipes also call for grated onion or garlic. Latkes are traditionally eaten for the Jewish Hanukkah festival. The oil for cooking the latkes is said to symbolize the oil from the Hanukkah story that kept the Second Temple of ancient Israel lit with a long-lasting flame. The event is celebrated as a miracle.

Latkes are so tasty, many non-Jewish or mixed religion families have adopted them as part of their winter celebrations.

Preparation time: 20 minutes
Cooking time: 6 minutes per batch
Makes 24 small latkes

Ingredients

2	large potatoes, peeled and coarsely grated	1	tablespoon vegetable oil + more for frying
1	small onion, grated	1½	tablespoons flour
1	teaspoon lemon juice		Salt and pepper to taste
2	eggs		Applesauce or sour cream (optional)

1. In a large bowl, combine potatoes, onion, lemon juice, eggs, and 1 tablespoon of oil. Mix well.
2. Mix salt, pepper, and flour, then blend in with the rest.
3. In a large heavy skillet, heat ¼ inch oil over medium-high heat.
4. By tablespoonfuls, spoon potato mixture into hot oil and flatten it with the back of the spoon. Brown on both sides, turning only once, about 3 minutes per side.
5. Drain latkes on paper towels.
6. Serve with applesauce or sour cream.

Making latkes isn't difficult, but these simple tips will ensure your success:

✡ Gather all your other ingredients before grating the potatoes so that they don't have time to turn brown.

✡ Latkes taste best when fried just before serving. If you're making a large batch, keep the first ones warm in the oven at 200°F while frying the remaining batter.

✡ For crispier latkes, flip them only once during cooking.

Pumpkin Harvest Bread

More than 85 percent of the world's canned pumpkin is processed in a small town in central Illinois. In 1978, the state's governor signed a proclamation naming Morton, Illinois, the Pumpkin Capital of the World.

Libby's first opened its pumpkin processing plant in Morton in 1960; in 1971 the plant was purchased by Nestlé. Every year, tons of pumpkins—all grown within a 150-mile radius of the plant—are processed there under the Libby's label.

The town celebrates the pumpkin at an annual festival each fall. It's there that festival-goers can sample dishes ranging from pumpkin pie and pumpkin doughnuts to pumpkin chili and pumpkin baked beans.

This moist loaf bread is perfect for Thanksgiving or winter holiday buffet tables. Of course, it's so yummy, you may want to make it at other times of the year as well.

Preparation time: 20 minutes
Cooking time: 60 to 70 minutes
Makes 2 large loaves

Ingredients

- 15-ounce can pure processed pumpkin
- 2 cups packed brown sugar
- 1 cup 100 percent natural apple juice
- 4 large eggs
- ¼ cup vegetable oil
- 2 teaspoons vanilla extract
- 4 cups flour
- 1 tablespoon pumpkin pie spice
- 2 teaspoons baking powder
- 1 teaspoon baking soda
- ¾ teaspoon salt
- 1 cup chopped nuts, divided

1. Preheat oven to 350°F.
2. Butter two 9 x 5-inch loaf pans. Sprinkle one tablespoon of flour inside each pan. Shake it to coat all surfaces with a light dusting. Turn the pan upside down over the sink and tap out the excess.
3. Mix pumpkin, sugar, juice, eggs, oil, and vanilla in a large bowl.

4. In another bowl, combine flour, pumpkin pie spice, baking powder, baking soda, and salt.
5. Stir flour mixture into pumpkin mixture. Mix well.
6. Add ¾ cup nuts and stir just until moistened.
7. Divide batter between the two loaf pans and sprinkle the remaining nuts over the loaves.
8. Bake 60 to 70 minutes or until wooden pick inserted in the center comes out clean.
9. Move pans to wire racks to cool completely.

appetizer (AA-peh-ty-zer)—Food or drink served before a meal or as the first course.

baking sheet—Also known as a cookie sheet, a thick tray, often insulated, that can be used for baking cookies and bars.

beat—To stir a mixture with a hard, rhythmic movement until it is smooth.

blend—To mix two or more ingredients until smooth and uniform.

boil—To cook until bubbles rise vigorously to the surface. The boiling point of water is 212°F at sea level.

brown—To cook food quickly in a pan on the stove or under a broiler to develop a brown surface and to seal in the natural juices.

brush—To spread food with butter, margarine, or egg using a small brush intended solely for food preparation.

chop—To cut food into small pieces with a knife or small cutting appliance.

coat—To roll foods in flour, nuts, sugar, or crumbs until all sides are evenly covered; or to dip first into beaten egg or milk, then cover with a specified coating.

combine—To mix various ingredients together.

core—To remove the center of a fruit, such as an apple or pear, or of a vegetable, such as a head of lettuce or cabbage. Coring eliminates seeds and tough centers.

cream—To whip or beat with a spoon or mixer until mixture is soft and fluffy. This term is often used to describe the combining of butter and sugar.

dice—To cut into small cubes of uniform size, usually about ¼ inch across.

dissolve—To make a dry substance break down completely in a liquid.

dust—To sprinkle a food or coat it lightly with flour, sugar, cornmeal, or cocoa powder.

fold—To gently blend a light ingredient, such as beaten egg whites, into a heavier ingredient by lifting from underneath with a spatula or spoon and then turning it over.

fry or **pan-fry**—To cook in a small amount of fat or oil on top of the stove.

garnish—To decorate a dish with a colorful piece of fresh fruit or vegetable.

grate—To rub on a grater (a tool with several sharp blades) causing the food to shred. Potatoes, carrots, and cheese are often grated.

knead (NEED)—To work and press dough with the heels of your hands until the dough becomes stretched and elastic.

pound—To flatten meats or poultry to a uniform thickness using a meat mallet. This tenderizes tough meat by breaking up connective tissues and allows for even cooking throughout.

preheat—To heat an oven to a stated temperature before using.

simmer—To cook in a liquid that is kept just below the boiling point.

whisk—To beat ingredients (such as cream, eggs, or sauces) with a fork or the looped wire utensil called a whisk so as to blend or incorporate air.

Books

Nissenberg, Sandra K. *The Everything Kids' Cookbook: From Mac 'n' Cheese to Double Chocolate Chip Cookies—All You Need to Have Some Finger Lickin' Fun*. Avon, MA: Adams Media, 2008.

Rau, Dana Meachen. *Food and Cooking in American History*. Milwaukee, WI: Weekly Reader Early Learning Library, 2007.

Tuminelly, Nancy. *Super Simple Snacks: Easy No-bake Recipes for Kids*. Edina, MN: ABDO Publisers, 2011.

Works Consulted

This book is based on the author's experiences living in the Midwest, and on the following sources:

Andrews, Glenn. *Food from the Heartland: The Cooking of America's Midwest*. New York: Prentice Hall, 1991.

Burckhardt, Ann. *Hot Dish Heaven: Classic Casseroles from Midwest Kitchens*. St. Paul: Minnesota Historical Society, 2006.

Favorite Recipes from Great Midwest Cooks. Des Moines, IA: Meredith, 1992.

Loyd, Jim. *Jim Loyd's Best of the Open Line Cookbook*. Cedar Rapids, IA: WMT Radio, 1968.

Mandel, Abby. *Celebrating the Midwestern Table: Real Food for Real Times*. New York: Doubleday, 1996.

Rombauer, Irma Von Starkloff, Marion Rombauer Becker, and Ethan Becker. *Joy of Cooking*. New York: Scribner, 2006.

On the Internet

Iowa Egg Producers
http://www.iowaegg.org

Iowa Honey Producers
http://www.abuzzaboutbees.com

Iowa Pork Producers
http://www.iowapork.org

Iowa Turkey Federation
http://www.iowaturkey.org

Maid-Rite Restaurants
http://www.maid-rite.com

Michigan Apple Growers
http://www.michiganapples.com

Minnesota Wild Rice
http://www.mnwildrice.com

Morton (Ill.) Pumpkin Festival
http://www.pumpkincapital.com/pumpkin-festival

National Popcorn Board
http://www.popcorn.org

Wisconsin Cheese Board
http://www.eatwisconsincheese.com

Wisconsin Cranberries
http://www.wiscran.org

Index

About the
AUTHOR

Mary Boone grew up on an Iowa farm, where she learned how to cook from her mom, Sue, and bake from her grandmother, Ruth. Over the years, Mary has worked as a food editor for several Midwest newspapers. She now lives in the Pacific Northwest but lets her cooking transport her back home on a regular basis.